GREATEST OF ALL TIME PLAYERS

G.O.A.T. BASEBALL PITCHERS

Alexander Lowe

Lerner Publications ◆ Minneapolis

SPORTS THRILLS MEET RESEARCH SKILLS

Lerner SPORTS

Free Database Trial: **lernersports.com**

Lerner Publications Company
An imprint of Lerner Publishing Group, Inc.
241 First Avenue North
Minneapolis, MN 55401 USA

For reading levels and more information, look up this title at www.lernerbooks.com.

Main body text set in Aptifer Sans LT Pro.
Typeface provided by Linotype AG.

Library of Congress Cataloging-in-Publication Data
Names: Lowe, Alexander, author.
Title: G.O.A.T. baseball pitchers / Alexander Lowe.
Other titles: Greatest of All Time baseball pitchers
Description: Minneapolis : Lerner Publications, [2022] | Series: Greatest of All Time Players (Lerner Sports) | Includes bibliographical references and index. | Audience: Ages 7–11 years | Audience: Grades 4–6 | Summary: "Pitchers can influence games more than any other player on the field. Read about the stats and championship moments of baseball's greatest pitchers. Then use what you learned to create your own top-10 list!"— Provided by publisher.
Identifiers: LCCN 2021017971 (print) | LCCN 2021017972 (ebook) | ISBN 9781728441092 (Library Binding) | ISBN 9781728448428 (Paperback) | ISBN 9781728444758 (eBook)
Subjects: LCSH: Pitchers (Baseball)—Juvenile literature. | Baseball—Miscellanea—Juvenile literature. | Baseball—History—Miscellanea—Juvenile literature. | Baseball players—Rating of.
Classification: LCC GV867.5 .L68 2022 (print) | LCC GV867.5 (ebook) | DDC 796.357092/2 [B]—dc23

LC record available at https://lccn.loc.gov/2021017971
LC ebook record available at https://lccn.loc.gov/2021017972

Manufactured in the United States of America
2-53208-49723-4/6/2022

TABLE OF CONTENTS

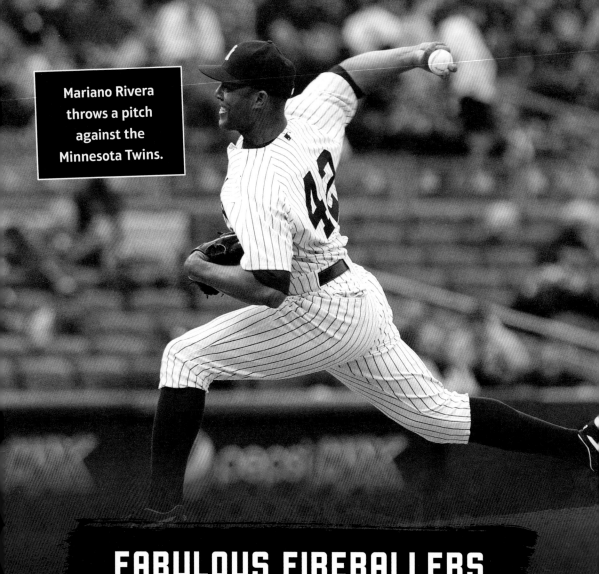

Mariano Rivera throws a pitch against the Minnesota Twins.

FABULOUS FIREBALLERS

On September 19, 2011, the New York Yankees were playing the Minnesota Twins. Mariano Rivera stepped onto the pitching mound. The count was no balls and two strikes. Rivera wound up for the pitch. He unleashed his famous cut fastball. It swept across the corner of the plate for a called strike three. The batter was out, and the game was over. Rivera became the all-time leader in saves in Major League Baseball (MLB).

FACTS AT A GLANCE

» **CY YOUNG** HOLDS THE MLB RECORD FOR CAREER WINS, WITH 511.

» **NOLAN RYAN** OFTEN THREW THE BALL MORE THAN 100 MILES (161 KM) PER HOUR.

» **SATCHEL PAIGE** THREW AS MANY AS 50 NO-HITTERS IN HIS CAREER.

» **RANDY JOHNSON** HOLDS THE RECORD FOR CAREER STRIKEOUTS BY A LEFT-HANDED PITCHER WITH 4,875.

MLB started in 1903. The game has changed in many ways since then. One of the biggest changes came in 1947. That year, Jackie Robinson (*right*) of the Brooklyn Dodgers became the first Black player to take the field in the league. Before then, no Black players were allowed to play. Black players played in the Negro Leagues before Robinson made history. Many of the greatest Black players didn't have the opportunity to play in MLB.

In baseball, every play begins when the pitcher throws the ball. The pitcher controls the speed of the game. The best pitchers can keep hitters from making solid contact with the ball. They can help their defense by keeping runners off base. But a bad game from a pitcher can also make it nearly impossible to win. That's why great pitchers are so valuable.

Randy Johnson pitched in six seasons for the Arizona Diamondbacks. Johnson is one of the tallest pitchers in MLB history.

Satchel Paige played his first MLB game with the Cleveland Indians in 1948. He became the first former Negro Leagues pitcher to pitch in the World Series when Cleveland won the 1948 title.

It can be hard to rank the best pitchers in baseball history. Many great athletes have played the position. Every baseball fan has an opinion on the greatest of all time (G.O.A.T.)!

Fans know that a pitcher is great when MLB changes the game's rules to make him less dominant. After Bob Gibson's 1968 season, the league was worried that teams were not scoring enough runs. That year, Gibson set a record with a 1.12 earned run average (ERA). That means he only gave up about one run for every nine innings he pitched. MLB lowered the mound and made the strike zone smaller in an effort to make sure pitchers did not have an unfair advantage.

In 1968, Gibson won the Most Valuable Player (MVP) award. A pitcher has to be incredible to win MVP. Position players such as outfielders usually win the award. To win MVP, a pitcher has to be more than just a good pitcher. They have to be the best player on the team at any position. Gibson also won two Cy Young Awards as the best pitcher in his league.

Gibson played in three World Series. He helped the St. Louis Cardinals win in 1964 and 1967, and Gibson was named World Series MVP both times. In total, Gibson pitched in nine World Series games. He pitched all nine innings in eight of those nine appearances.

BOB GIBSON STATS

Wins		251
ERA		2.91
Strikeouts		3,117
Innings Pitched		3,884

NOLAN RYAN

Nolan Ryan was the king of the no-hitter. Throughout his career, he pitched seven of them. No other player has thrown more than five. Only four other players have even thrown more than two. When Ryan was having his best games, he was absolutely unhittable.

Ryan made his mark with a blazing fastball. That pitch was consistently over 100 miles (161 km) per hour. Some say that he threw as fast as 108 miles (174 km) per hour. When his fastball was humming, batters didn't stand a chance.

Ryan did not always have the best control of his pitches. If he did, he might have been the greatest pitcher of all time. He walked more than four batters per nine innings pitched, which is far higher than most other great pitchers. Still, his dominance when he was at his best is more than enough to make up for the amount of players he walked.

NOLAN RYAN STATS

⚾	Wins	324
⚾	ERA	3.19
⚾	Strikeouts	5,714
⚾	Innings Pitched	5,386

CHRISTY MATHEWSON

Christy Mathewson was one of the first MLB pitching stars. One of his best seasons came in 1905 for the New York Giants. That year, he won 31 games and had a 1.28 ERA.

The best players step up when it matters the most. In baseball, the most important games take place in the World Series. In the 1905 series, Mathewson pitched complete-game shutouts in three games. That means he threw all nine innings of each game without giving up a single run. His performance was a big factor in the Giants' win.

Mathewson was a star throughout his career. He was known for being cool under pressure and always coming through for his team. Stepping up when it matters the most is the sign of a true G.O.A.T.

CHRISTY MATHEWSON STATS

🏐	Wins	373
🏐	ERA	2.13
🏐	Strikeouts	2,502
🏐	Innings Pitched	4,788

CY YOUNG

Many of baseball's G.O.A.T. pitchers are Cy Young Award winners. It is no surprise that this award is named after one of the greatest pitchers to play the sport. Each season, the award recognizes the best pitcher in the American League and the National League. Young is widely considered to be the first pitching superstar in MLB history.

In Young's era, starting pitchers did not play once every five games like they do now. Many pitchers were on the mound more frequently and threw complete games. Young did this better than anyone. He started 815 games during his career and pitched complete games in 749 of them. Young never seemed to get tired. He wore down opposing teams with his ability to keep throwing hard right down to the last pitch of the game.

Young is the all-time leader in games won. His 511 career wins are nearly 100 wins ahead of the second-place pitcher. That is a record that will probably never be broken.

CY YOUNG STATS

Wins	511
ERA	2.63
Strikeouts	2,803
Innings Pitched	7,356

SATCHEL PAIGE

Satchel Paige was the greatest pitcher in history who did not have a chance to play his best years in MLB. Paige played most of his career before MLB allowed Black players to join, so he pitched in the Negro Leagues. By the time he played his first game for the Cleveland Indians in 1948, he was around 41 years old. His best days were behind him.

Unfortunately, statistics in the Negro Leagues were not always recorded. But Paige's Negro Leagues statistics are legendary. Experts estimate that he had over 2,000 victories in the 2,500 games he pitched. He threw as many as 50 no-hitters. He once won three games in a single day.

We may never know exactly how great Paige's early numbers were. But even without knowing the statistics from his Negro Leagues career, Paige was one of the greatest of all time.

SATCHEL PAIGE STATS

Wins	28
ERA	3.29
Strikeouts	288
Innings Pitched	476

RANDY JOHNSON

Batters were scared of Randy Johnson before he even threw a pitch. He was almost 7 feet (2.1 m) tall. Johnson's long legs and arms meant that his pitches seemed to cross home plate before the batter could react. Throw in the fact that his fastball could reach 102 miles (164 km) per hour, and Johnson was nearly unhittable.

Johnson was known for his ability to strike out batters. He has the second most strikeouts in MLB history. He also leads all left-handed pitchers in strikeouts. Johnson won the Cy Young Award five times.

But Johnson was more than just a hard-throwing pitcher. He could control the location of his pitches and he was fit enough to throw many innings. He won over 300 games in his career, a feat only 24 pitchers have accomplished. Johnson is the greatest left-handed pitcher of all time.

RANDY JOHNSON STATS

Wins		303
ERA		3.29
Strikeouts		4,875
Innings Pitched		4,135

MARIANO RIVERA

Mariano Rivera is the best closer of all time. Most of the greatest pitchers are starters. Closers come into games near the end to finish off the other team. They usually only pitch when the game is close. No one was better at securing wins for his team than Rivera.

Rivera came into the league in 1995. The next year, he helped the Yankees win the World Series. His success only grew from there. He racked up saves year after year. By the time he retired, he was the all-time MLB leader in saves.

Rivera was best known for his cut fastball. There were entire games where he did not throw any other pitch. Most pitchers throw more than one type of pitch to keep hitters guessing. But Rivera did not need variety to stump his opponents. They often knew exactly what was coming and still could not make contact with Rivera's pitches. There may never be another closer with a greater impact on the outcome of games than Rivera had.

MARIANO RIVERA STATS

⚾	Wins	82
⚾	ERA	2.21
⚾	Strikeouts	1,173
⚾	Saves	652

PEDRO MARTINEZ

For seven years in the middle of his career, Pedro Martinez might have pitched better than any other player in MLB history. During that time, Martinez averaged more than 11 strikeouts per nine innings.

Martinez had an incredible changeup. Some say it was the best pitch of all time. Martinez's changeup was possible because of his dominant fastball. Batters would be expecting the fastball. They would not have a chance to react to a changeup that was 10 miles (16 km) per hour slower than they were expecting. Then they had to deal with the ball breaking toward the bottom of the strike zone. Martinez's fastball and changeup combination made him almost impossible to hit.

Martinez won three Cy Young Awards. He finished in the top five of Cy Young voting another four times. He also helped the Boston Red Sox win the World Series in 2004. Before that, the team had not won an MLB championship since 1918.

PEDRO MARTINEZ STATS

⚾	Wins	219
⚾	ERA	2.93
⚾	Strikeouts	3,154
⚾	Innings Pitched	2,827

WALTER JOHNSON

Walter Johnson had a long, dominant career. From the time he joined the league at 19 until his late 30s, Johnson was the best pitcher in the game.

Johnson's 1913 season is the best a pitcher has ever had. He won 36 games that year and had an ERA of 1.14. He struck out 243 batters that season. It was one of eight straight years when he led the league in strikeouts.

Johnson won the MVP award twice in his career, once when he was 26 and then again when he was 37. There were plenty of seasons in between when he easily could have won the award. It is impossible to say how Johnson would have done against modern competition. But judging by how dominant he was, he would have been a star in any era.

WALTER JOHNSON STATS

Wins		417
ERA		2.17
Strikeouts		3,509
Innings Pitched		5,914

GREG MADDUX

The 1990s was a decade of big-muscled sluggers and pitchers. Batters hit the ball far and pitchers threw the ball hard. But Greg Maddux was different. He was never the hardest thrower on his team. His fastest pitches were only about 93 miles (150 km) per hour. But even without a blazing fastball, Maddux constantly found ways to catch batters off guard.

Maddux was nicknamed The Professor. He earned this name by being smarter than his opponents. He always seemed to know exactly where to throw the ball. He did not have nearly as many strikeouts as some other great pitchers, but it made no difference. He was able to throw the ball where the batter could only make weak contact for an easy out.

Maddux won four straight Cy Young Awards from 1992 to 1995. He was also an incredible fielder. He won 18 Gold Gloves as the best fielder at his position. Maddux holds the record across all positions for the most Gold Gloves won.

GREG MADDUX STATS

⚾	Wins	355
⚾	ERA	3.16
⚾	Strikeouts	3,371
⚾	Innings Pitched	5,008

EVEN MORE G.O.A.T.

There have been many other great players who were pitchers. Choosing the 10 greatest of all time is difficult. Here are another 10 players who nearly made the top-10 list.

No. 11	ROGER CLEMENS
No. 12	SANDY KOUFAX
No. 13	TOM SEAVER
No. 14	WARREN SPAHN
No. 15	JOHN SMOLTZ
No. 16	FERGIE JENKINS
No. 17	MAX SCHERZER
No. 18	CLAYTON KERSHAW
No. 19	TREVOR HOFFMAN
No. 20	TOM GLAVINE

YOUR
G.O.A.T.

It's your turn to make a G.O.A.T. list about baseball pitchers. Start by doing research. Consider the rankings in this book. Then check out the Learn More section on page 31. Explore the books and websites to learn more about baseball pitchers of the past and present.

You can search online for more information about great players too. Check with a librarian, who may have other resources for you. You might even try reaching out to baseball teams or players to see what they think.

Once you're ready, make your list of the greatest pitchers of all time. Then ask people you know to make G.O.A.T. lists and compare them. Do you have players no one else listed? Are you missing anybody your friends think is important? Talk it over, and try to convince them that your list is the G.O.A.T.!

GLOSSARY

changeup: a slow pitch thrown with the same motion as a fastball in order to trick the batter

closer: a relief pitcher who usually finishes games

complete game: when the starting pitcher pitches all nine innings of a game

count: the number of balls and strikes charged to a batter during one turn

cut fastball: a fastball thrown with sideways spin so that it moves left or right as it nears the plate

Cy Young Award: an award presented each year to the best pitcher in the American League and the National League

earned run average (ERA): the average number of earned runs (runs scored without the benefit of an error) per game scored against a pitcher

Gold Glove: an award presented each year to the best fielder at each position

Negro Leagues: former baseball leagues that were made up of Black people and other people of color

no-hitter: when a pitcher doesn't give up a hit in a complete game

save: when a relief pitcher protects a team's lead

shutout: when a starting pitcher throws nine innings and does not give up a run

walk: an advance to first base awarded to a player who during a turn at bat takes four pitches that are outside the strike zone

LEARN MORE

Baseball Hall of Fame
https://baseballhall.org/

Fishman, Jon M. *Baseball's G.O.A.T.: Babe Ruth, Mike Trout, and More.* Minneapolis: Lerner Publications, 2020.

Monson, James. *Behind the Scenes Baseball.* Minneapolis: Lerner Publications, 2020.

Murray, Hallie. *Satchel Paige: Legendary Pitcher.* New York: Enslow Publishing, 2020.

Ranking the 25 Best Baseball Players of All Time
https://bleacherreport.com/articles/2699455-ranking-the-25-best-baseball-players-of-all-time

25 Best Starting Pitchers of All Time
https://athlonsports.com/mlb/25-greatest-starting-pitchers-major-league-baseball-history

INDEX

PHOTO ACKNOWLEDGMENTS

Image credits: Christof Koepsel/Staff/pngimg.com, p.3; Nick Laham/Staff/Getty Images, p.4; Everett Collection Historical/Alamy, p.5; Todd Warshaw/Staff/Getty Images, p.6; Patti McConville/Alamy, p.7; TSN/Icon SMI/Newscom, p.8; Sporting News Archives/Icon//Newscom, p.9; Ai Wire Photo Service/Newscom, p.10; Cliff Welch/Icon SMI/Newscom, p.11; JT Vintage/ZUMA Press/Newscom, p.12; FPG / Staff/Getty Images, p.13; Everett Collection/Newscom, p.14; Everett Collection/ Newscom, p.15; Dwight E. Dolan/ZUMAPRESS/Newscom, p.16; TSN/Icon SMI/ Newscom, p.17; Jed Jacobsohn/Staff/Getty Images, p.18; Brian Bahr/Staff/Getty Images, p.19; Ezra Shaw/Staff/Getty Images, p.20; Al Bello/Staff/Getty Images, p.21; Jeff Gross/Staff/Getty Images, 22; Doug Benc/Staff/Getty Images, p.23; Everett Collection Inc/Alamy, p.24; FPG/Staff/Getty Images, p.25; Jonathan Daniel/ Stringer/Getty Images, p.26; Jeff Gross/Staff/Getty Images, p.27; Nadezhda Shpiiakina/Shutterstock, Background

Cover: Nick Laham/Staff/Getty Images; Jeff Gross/Staff/Getty Images; Jonathan Daniel/Staff/Getty Images; Nadezhda Shpiiakina/Shutterstock